A New Dawn

Ardian Newell

THIS BOOK IS DEDICATED to the piece of my heart I call Auntie Mar. If you didn't lose Deacon, I don't think I would have had these thoughts. If you didn't suggest I put these thoughts in a book I probably never would have. This book is literally because of you Auntie Mar. Gawd is good.

The caterpillar's death can't be rushed so the butterfly can get his wings. The caterpillar's mortality brings about a beautiful thing. Death brings about a change, but everything in nature eventually learns to flourish in it's time.

A NEW DAWN

A new dawn, a new sun
A brand new day
A life that will never be the same...

When you awake in the morning
and don't see me beside you
Be encouraged by knowing that though
I'm no longer in view, I'll always live
inside of you

When you feel the void left
by my empty space
Remember what it felt like to
be held by my embrace
May the sweet memories of you
and me make your heart sing
a beautiful melody

When you start to feel a loneliness
you've never felt before,
may your days and nights be made
better by a comforting assurance that
I will always be present

I'll be with you every step of the way,
though the physical journey I'll no
longer take

When you need a word to cheer you,
think about the jokes exchanged between
us and all the laughter shared
May our conversations continue

like a whisper that speaks quietly in your ear

When you begin to miss me unbearably,
think about those times we held each
other close enough to feel two heartbeats
and never let those moments go
Use them to caress your blues away
so that the memory can put a smile
across your face

When your arms long to hold me and
I'm not anywhere near, may your need for
the physical me be quenched by knowing
I wouldn't have left your grasp empty
under any other circumstance
If I could have held you longer, I would
have, ten times over, just so the touch of
yesterday could linger

When your ears strain to hear the sound
of my voice and time erases my
fleshy existence, may you find comfort
in knowing that though I am distant,
sound travels any wave length

The music we've made will always remain
The soundtrack of our lives will always play
Put the good times on repeat and in those
moments I will always speak

When your hands struggle to deal with
the absence of my touch, may you feel
the love transferred each time our hands
were clasped together

So that you may know that though
I now rest in peace
Our love was sealed with the kiss of
eternity and forever yours I'll be

I know there will be tears and pain
you don't understand
I hate to see you cry
But a new dawn has come, bringing with it
a new sun

Sorry I can't stay

Goodbye my love
Hello to a new day

You have to go through the valley of the shadow of death to experience the mountaintop of new mercies. The valleys in life are places in this journey, not final destinations. It rains hard in the valley and gets really dark at night. The sun however will rise.

Sunshine will always break through the clouds. Even on the darkest and gloomiest days there is always light. Look for the ray of sunlight that breaks through the clouds and sets everything around it aglow.

To rise with the sun means to stand as tall as you can, and to face the day with an open heart. To rise with the sun is a privilege and an opportunity to spread love and warmth like sun rays. When the day is beautiful it is a day full of opportunities to walk in light, spread love and create beauty.

Today is still a gift regardless of what the day may bring. It requires

you to be fully present in whatever moment you find yourself in.

FLICKERS AND FLAMES

If life is nothing but a flicker
that can be extinguished in a second,
may the flame of love burn bright
For love is eternal and a single flame
can set the world ablaze

A heart may burn with a yearning
for loved ones lost, but remember
even gold is tried in the fire
Purified and made the better
Broken hearts with time can be mended
Bound together by memories that will
last forever

Love is always worth it, regardless
of time spent together
For it never diminishes but rather
replenishes the soul
As long as there is love, there is an
opportunity for every human to grow

Love's eternal flame can illuminate
the darkest night
It's radiation warm the days that
seem like ice
Love is a guiding light in darkness
For life is just a flicker that burns like a
flame as long as love remains

A life may fade but the joy, love, and the feeling a life creates

is everlasting. The evidence of a life that was, never goes

away as long as someone is alive to remember.

Love is a jewel that makes life beautiful. It sparkles and shines to change

our lives for the better. As long as there is love, a jewel can never lose its

luster. It will continue to shine like a light when you need it the most.

The power of love is it affects the giver and the receiver. One must be open to learning from love and experience all love has to offer. One must be willing to share love freely without knowing the return. One must be willing to hold on to true love and be open to love when love presents itself in new forms.

Happiness is not dependent on a day. Days come and go, bringing with them different situations and different emotions. Happiness instead is rooted in love, watered with joy, and bears fruit through memories.

Sometimes you have to go and put yourself in the middle of love, so you can be surrounded by it. The force is strongest by the epicenter.

THE FLIGHT OF A SONGBIRD

When a songbird sings
Those who hear the sound,
stop and marvel in the joy
it's voice brings

The pretty bird may then
be placed in a cage
so the power of it's range
can be displayed

Though done with the
best intent, our act
of clipping a songbird's wings
are selfish
For beauty can't be contained
forever and songbirds are
created to soar

Once released, even if
reluctantly, the trajectory
of the songbird's journey
may be unknown
However the songbird will
find it's way home
Connected to the composer
of it's cherished song

Though heartbroken,
one must bid the songbird
adieu with instructions
such as these to adhere to

Fly high songbird and
set your spirit free
Let the wings of a dove
take your voice so the world too
can join in the song you sing

Ride the wave of a beautiful
melody that swells in harmony
like the waves that crest in the sea

With lyrics of endless love,
peace, and light, let your
voice ring in the heavens
So when it rains on Earth,
those who remember your song
can hear the angles sing

Set eternity to music
Like a favorite song that
never gets old
Sweet to the ear with each
listen
A candy coated rendering that
drips with honey and soothes
one's soul

Fly high sweet songbird
Touch the top of the clouds
with each flap of your wings
Paint the sky in beautiful hues
so that each sunrise and sunset
will bring memories of you

Let your voice be carried in

the wind
So that each blowing breeze
may cause those who knew
you, to stop and listen
If they choose to

When caged, the warmth of
your spirit caused others
to bask in your glow
Now released, you must
sow beauty where ever you go

Abide in love. For where there is love, there is God. Where there is love, you'll have everything you need.

Tears flow from loves wellspring. They are never anything to be ashamed about for they are signs that you've had a love experience. Even in heartbreak, the root of heartbreak is a love that taught you something or left an impact on your life. If you need to cry, cry, and do so without apology for there is healing power in running water.

It's okay to not feel okay. It's okay to not feel your best and

maybe even be off. It's okay to cry and it's even okay to be

vulnerable. In vulnerability there is strength. In these

emotions there is connection to every living thing.

There is wonder in darkness for in darkness,

the smallest light shines the brightest.

YOU LEFT US

You left us...

And though the sense of abandonment
will eventually fade
The truth of the matter is, it's been days
since you graced us with your presence
Hours since you last smiled and countless
minutes since the last time you held us in
an embrace
You left our grasp empty for what will
become the rest of eternity

It seems hard to accept that time with
you in it, is now past tense
That time is now based on yesterdays and
in our hearts is where you'll remain

You left us alone to take the next step
as we attempt to navigate life without
you by our side
Wandering and feeling our way like the
blind who have no guide

You left us with an uneven trade
For no amount of bartering can replace
this level of heartbreak
If these tears could speak, they would speak
of love lost with each silent stream

There's an emptiness where you used to be
An unfamiliar territory, for you were
always there like a guiding star

And now clouds cover the sky
Leaving nothing but a black night
Dark days are ahead that must be faced
Which wouldn't be the case, if only you
stayed

But you left us...

Selfishly we would change your fate
If only to behold your face for one more day
We would make every second count and
set the clocks back before time ran out
So this feeling of you with us could never leave

In actuality, this could never be reality
For every day that passes without you is
a constant reminder that you left us
You left us with tears
With lessons and memories we'll cherish forever
But you left us...

For the better

The essence and soul of a person never dies. We don't lose the people we love. We experience them. As a result of human experience, people who are loved are able to transcend space and time as long as a heart beats that carries them along.

When you make room in your heart for another person, that space is always reserved for them. That space may feel like an open wound in their departure, however all wounds heal over time. The power of the human body is that it will heal itself as long as the human is open to loving, laughing, learning, and growing. Flowers open to bloom and shrivel up and wither to die. Reserve and sanctify the space for loved ones lost but remain open to life and all it brings.

Love has the power to break you and rebuild you in a way that

makes you wiser, stronger, and made better for taking apart.

Love is life and to love is to live fully and completely.

AFTER THE RIVER DRIES

After the rain comes
the sun
But what happens after
the course of the river
has been run and what was
is no longer?
Like a whisper that
fades into the air...

The pathway of the river remains
dry, cracked, and scorched
Raw, and baring the earth

After the river dries,
what is left behind?

Be it the multiple rivers of tears
cried from coast to coast
Flowing from continent to continent
Gently streaming down
cheeks like the faucet which leaks
Or the deluge of sorrow
sprung from the depth of despair
Where broken hearts are
in need of repair

How does one move forward
despite the memory of
washed away yesterdays
and the residue of tears
permanently left on
one's face?

For the course of the river
has been run
Impossible to be deterred
No matter how much
it hurts

What happens when
the voices of the people
are quieted?

And demands for justice
no longer echo like
the liberty bell has rung
Or reverberate through
the streets
But parents are still
burying their daughters
and sons
Over senseless hate
While waiting patiently
for love to overcome
However love lost
won't bring lost loved ones
home

After the river dries,
what is left behind?

Does the river run in
reverse, washing over
every ounce of previous
hurt?
Making the pain go away
So your tomorrows will

be better, never to cause
the pain of yesterday
Erasing valuable lessons learned
and eradicating hard-fought
victories earned

If time stood still
and the river remained
peaceful and serene,
growth would be denied
for every human being
The constant change in
the swell of the river
would be lost and the force
of the river for better and worse
would weaken
And never would the tide rise

The natural order is progression
To grow, learn, experience
the hurt and be made the better

But yet the earth remains
dry, cracked, and scorched
Raw to the core

Meet me at the place
where the river meets
the sun
So we can rise above
the destruction done

Everything broken, from bones to the finest of crystal, can be repaired.
Broken hearts can also be repaired with tender loving care and as
much time as needed. When things are broken and then repaired,
they never quite go back to the way they were. Instead a different
version of what was, now exist as a testament to the power of repair.

Moving forward does not mean forgetting the past or ignoring the hurt that has occurred. Moving forward does not mean knowing the next step, the direction of progress, or even how to proceed, but proceeding anyway.

Situations will come that shake your foundation to the core.

Everything happens to make your roots stronger so that

you can continue to withstand what comes your way.

Submission does not mean losing control even though the world may appear to be spinning out of control around you. In life everything submits to something and when life is over, life too submits to death. There is power in submission for times of transition bring about transformation.

The baby who stumbles may grow up one day and run a marathon. The eagle who falls out the nest is going to soar. The colt that wobbles may grow up and win the Kentucky Derby. Growth happens in baby steps. There will be setbacks, but continue forward.

Gratitude can't be limited to a certain season or a certain period of time. There are so many things, great and small, to be thankful for every day. When you remain in gratitude, for the lessons, for the blessings, for even just the ability to feel, you can remain in a place where there is fulfillment.

In stillness, God speaks the loudest. In brokenness,

God does His best repairing.

STILL

Winds
Rains
Storms came
And yet the tree
remained

One more day
One more chance
Change is constant
And yet the tree
remained

Mountains high
Valleys low
Moments that transcend
the soul
And yet the tree
remained

Laughter
Tears
Joy
Despair
And yet the tree
remained

Every rainy day isn't a storm. Sometimes it's just a

little watering to help the growing process.

Some days there is progress and some days there are setbacks. Some days there are moments when you feel strong and powerful. Some days there are moments of vulnerability that seem like defeat. Some days the sun shines brightly and some days the clouds block the view. Some days laughter may fill your heart. Some days tears leave your heart feeling dehydrated and in need of care. Some days you might have more than enough and some days you might just need a little more. Some days are better than others but every day is an opportunity for better.

Both sorrow and laughter make the heart strong. It is life's

way of creating balance and God's way of refining you.

To find yourself in joy is to find yourself in a place where you can enjoy all that life has to offer. Life is lived out between highs and lows such as laughter and tears, love and heartbreak, disappointment and elation, and success and failures. If you can find yourself in joy in those moments, you will find there is still so much that makes life enjoyable.

Life is for the living. For sharing, laughing, loving, and forgiving. For growing, learning, and teaching. For giving and receiving, for hugging and holding, for relating. Life is beautiful when being or doing. If you haven't done anything yet today that makes life worth living, take a moment to do something to enhance your existence.

When you allow love to bloom fully and completely in your life, you will experience a spring in your step like never before. Love makes the sunshine brighter, heals previous hurt, and positively affects the loved and the lover. Everything flourishes when love is involved. Walk in love everywhere you go so others can follow in your footsteps.

Sometimes when you are in a place you've never been before, all you can do is take it one step at a time. Finding your bearings is hard and it takes time. The pathway to this day may have been filled with uncertainty, watered with tears, and unbearable pain. You made it to this day by taking one step and then another. Tomorrow will come, and just like you have since learning how to walk, you'll take one step and take another.

Sunshine warms the heart, soul, and body. It is God's gift after the rain.